CAROLS FOR
SUPPLE[

EDITOR: MICHAEL PERRY
SUPPLEMENT EDITOR: DAVID ILIFF

Hodder & Stoughton
LONDON SYDNEY AUCKLAND TORONTO

Also from Jubilate Hymns, published by Hodder and Stoughton:

Carols for Today – Music Edition
Carols for Today – Words Edition
Hymns for Today's Church
Church Family Worship
Psalms for Today
Songs from the Psalms

Copyright Information

Every effort to trace copyright holders and to obtain permission has been made; the publishers would welcome details of any errors or omissions. Corrections will be incorporated into future editions. This title is available in the USA from Hope Publishing Company, Carol Stream, Illinois 60188, USA.

British Library Cataloguing in Publication Data

Carols for today supplement: Jubilate Hymns
  1. Carols, English
  I. Perry, Michael   II. Iliff, David
  783.6'552   M1738

ISBN 0 340 53775 2

Copyright © 1990 by Michael Perry and David Iliff. First printed in 1990. All rights reserved. No part of this publication may be reproduced or transmitted in any form or by any means, electronically or mechanically, including photocopying, recording, or any information storage or retrieval system, without prior permission from the publisher and individual copyright holders. Printed in Great Britain for Hodder and Stoughton Limited, Mill Road, Dunton Green, Sevenoaks, Kent by St Edmundsbury Press, Bury St Edmunds, Suffolk. Set by Barnes Music Engraving Limited, East Sussex. Hodder and Stoughton Editorial Office: 47, Bedford Square, London WC1B 3DP.

CONTENTS

	Page
Preface	1
Section 1: Arrangements and Descants	2
Section 2: Introductions	70
Section 3: Instrumental Parts	77
Legal Information	99
First Lines, Titles and Original Sources Index	100

PREFACE

This book is designed to enrich further some of the material found in *Carols for Today*.

The first section contains new arrangements and descants which a choir may use to turn a straight congregational item into an anthem or to add a splash of colour to the final verse of a congregational item.

The second section, introductions, also enables an unadorned carol to become something special.

Instruments are much more often evident in churches now, and the instrumental parts in the third section will, used with discretion, add greatly to the effect of many of the carols.

Choir directors are urged to use this Supplement and *Carols for Today* with imagination and to adapt items to suit particular local circumstances. The medium must always be the servant of the message: the good news of Christ's incarnation.

David Iliff

SECTION 1: ARRANGEMENTS AND DESCANTS

1A   O come, O come, Emmanuel

Veni Emmanuel

Arrangement for choir and organ

1. O come, O come, Emmanuel and ransom captive Israel who mourns in lonely exile here until the Son of God draws near: Rejoice, rejoice! Emmanuel shall come to you, O Israel.

2. O come, true Branch of Jesse, free your children from this tyranny; from depths of hell your

3. O come, bright Day-break, come and cheer our spirits by your advent here; dispel the long night's

1A – O come, O come, Emmanuel

One or more verses may be used in conjunction with
the congregational version in *Carols for Today*.
See also page 79 for trumpet part for congregational version of this carol.

Music: from a fifteenth-century French missal
arranged © Merion Powell

Words: from the Latin (thirteenth century)
J M Neale (1818–1866) and others
© in this version Jubilate Hymns †

2 Come, O long-expected Jesus

Cross of Jesus

Added descant for verse 4

1 Come, O long-expected Jesus,
  born to set your people free!
  from our fears and sins release us,
  Christ in whom our rest shall be.

2 Israel's strength and consolation,
  born salvation to impart;
  dear desire of every nation,
  joy of every longing heart:

3 Born your people to deliver,
  born a child and yet a king;
  born to reign in us for ever,
  now your gracious kingdom bring:

4 By your own eternal Spirit
  rule in all our hearts alone;
  by your all-sufficient merit
  raise us to your glorious throne.

Music: J Stainer (1840–1901)
descant © Robin Sheldon

Words: C Wesley (1707–1788)
© in this version Jubilate Hymns †

O come, our world's Redeemer 5

Splendour
Added descant for verse 5

1. O come, our world's Redeemer, come! Let every age astonished be that God should grace the Virgin's womb and take our frail humanity.

2. For not by mortal will or power, but by the Holy Spirit's breath the seed of heaven comes to flower, the Word made flesh is found on earth.

3. He comes, for whom creation yearns, to face the realms of death alone; and to the Father he returns to gain a kingdom and a throne.

4. He comes to triumph over wrong
   and bring us captive back to heaven;
   for in our weakness he is strong,
   and for his sake we are forgiven.

5. O come, our world's Redeemer, come!
   Your manger shines upon our night –
   so let the voice of doubt be dumb,
   for none shall quench this glorious light!

This carol may be used effectively at the beginning of an Advent service in the following arrangement:
   Verse 1: *mp* Solo (unaccompanied)
   Verse 2: *mp* Upper voices in unison (accompanied)
   Verse 3: *mf* Lower voices in unison (accompanied)
   Verse 4: *f* Full harmony (unaccompanied)
   Verse 5: *f* Full unison with descant (accompanied)
See also page 80 for trumpet part.

Music: M Praetorius (1571–1621)
descant © David Iliff/Jubilate Hymns †

Words: from the Latin
© Michael Perry/Jubilate Hymns †

18A – Joy to the world

18A – Joy to the world

18A – Joy to the world

See also page 84 for trumpet part for congregational version of this carol.

Music: L Mason (1792–1872)
based on a theme by G F Handel (1685–1759)
arranged © Merion Powell

Words: I Watts (1674–1748)

The people who in darkness walked 20

Dundee

Added descant for verse 5

4 His name shall be the prince of peace,
  eternally adored;
  most wonderful of counsellors,
  the great and mighty Lord.

5 His peace and righteous government
  shall over all extend;
  on judgement and on justice based,
  his reign shall never end.

Music: *Scottish Psalter*, Edinburgh (1615)
descant © Anthony Greening

Words: from Isaiah 9
J Morison (1750–1798)
© in this version Jubilate Hymns †

21A The darkness turns to dawn

Saigon

Arrangement and fauxbourdon for choir

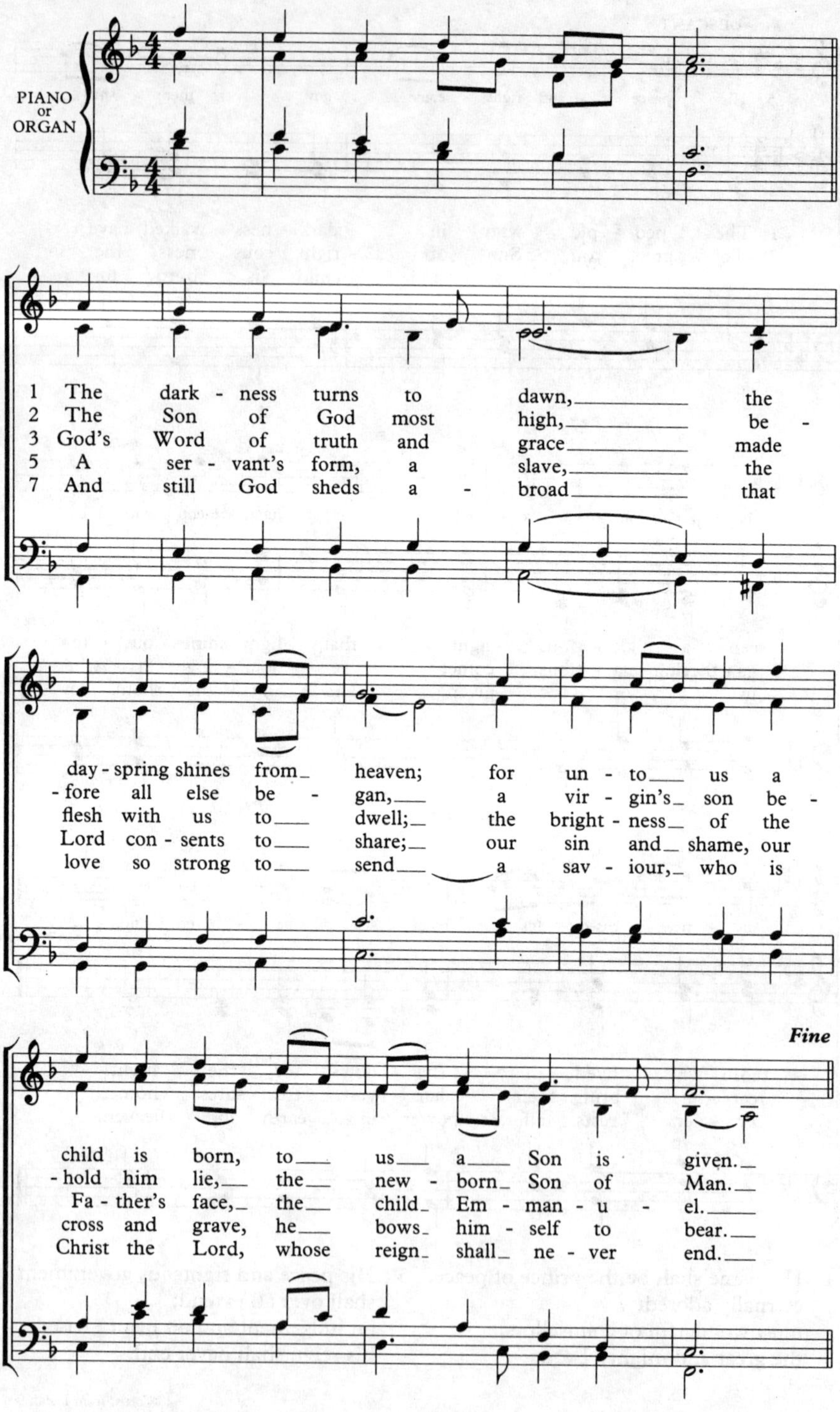

1 The darkness turns to dawn, the day-spring shines from heaven; for unto us a child is born, to us a Son is given.
2 The Son of God most high, before all else began, a virgin's son behold him lie, the new-born Son of Man.
3 God's Word of truth and grace made flesh with us to dwell; the brightness of the Father's face, the child Emmanuel.
5 A servant's form, a slave, the Lord consents to share; our sin and shame, our cross and grave, he bows himself to bear.
7 And still God sheds abroad that love so strong to send a saviour, who is Christ the Lord, whose reign shall never end.

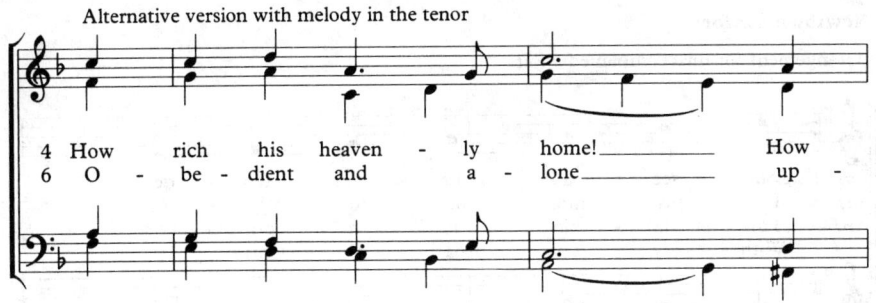

Music: © Norman Warren/Jubilate Hymns †
alternative version arranged © David Iliff/Jubilate Hymns †

Words: © Timothy Dudley-Smith

37A Come, see a little tender babe

Newtown Linford

Arrangement for unaccompanied choir

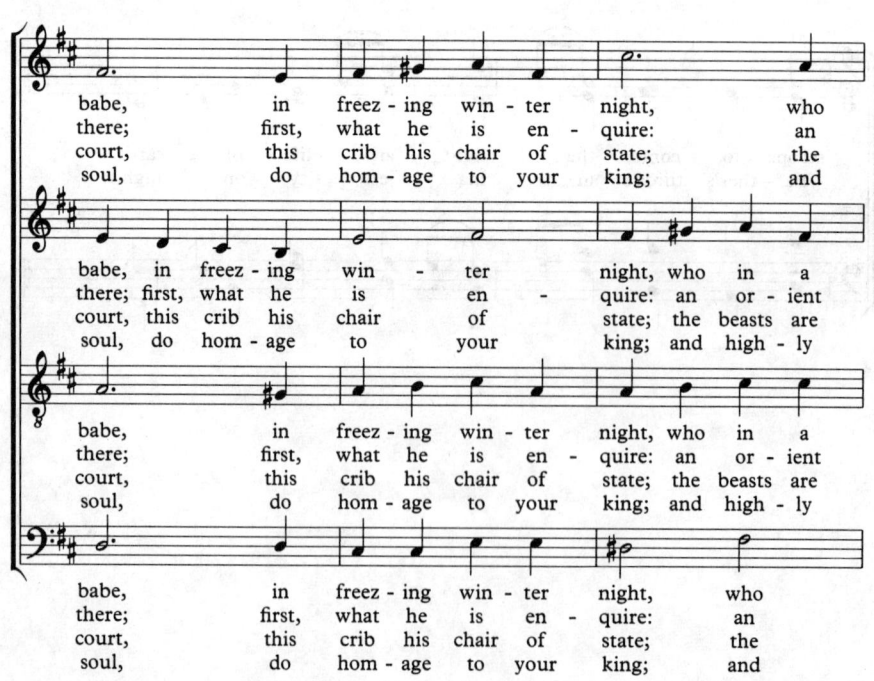

37A – Come, see a little tender babe

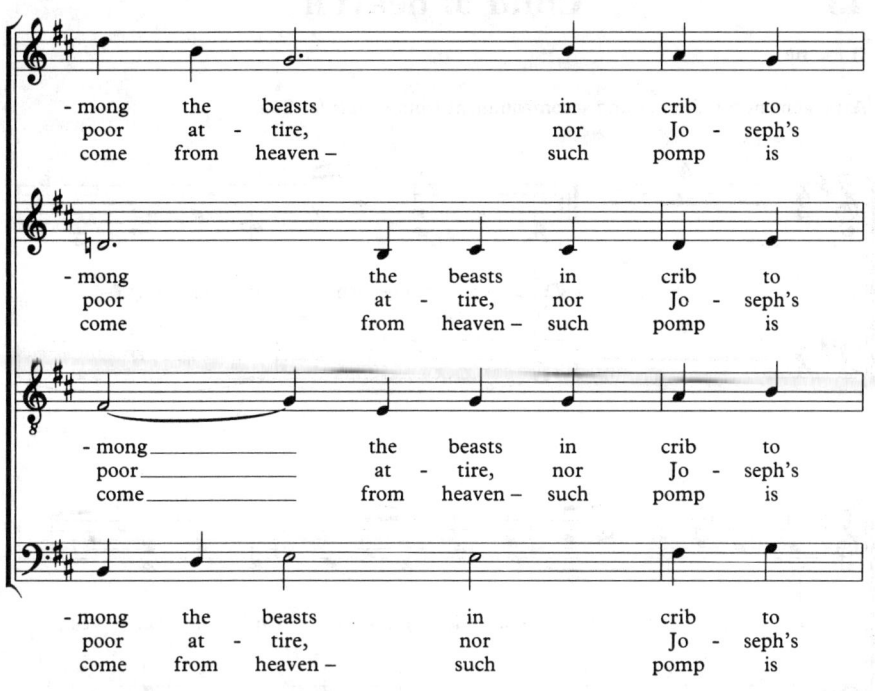
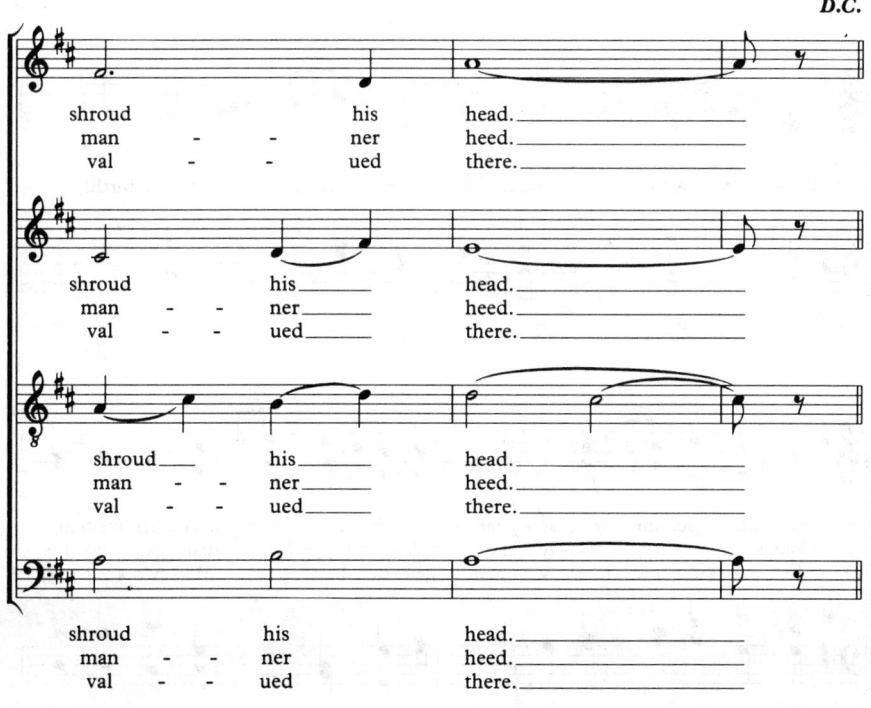

Words: R Southwell (1561–1595)
Music: © Peter White/Jubilate Hymns †
© in this version Word & Music/Jubilate Hymns †

43   Child of heaven

Il est né

Arrangement for choir (using accompaniment from *Carols for Today*)

♩ = 132

Child of hea-ven— born on earth—

let the— mu-sic— sound his prais-es: Child of hea-ven—

born on earth— sing to greet the— sav-iour's birth!

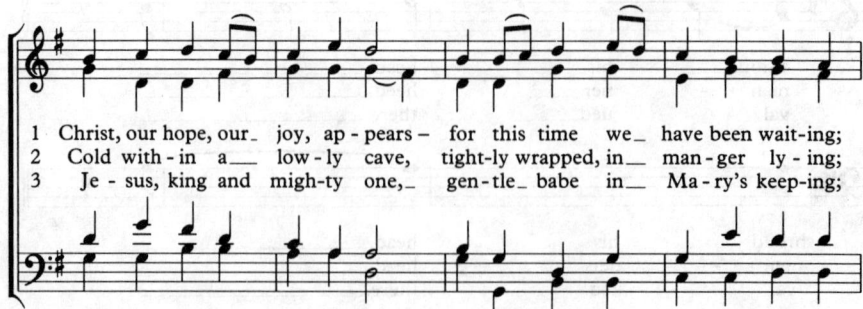

1 Christ, our hope, our— joy, ap-pears— for this time we— have been wait-ing;
2 Cold with-in a— low-ly cave, tight-ly wrapped, in— man-ger ly-ing;
3 Je-sus, king and migh-ty one,— gen-tle— babe in— Ma-ry's keep-ing;

Suggested performance:
    Chorus: Upper voices only
    Verse 1: 4-part harmony hummed
    Chorus: 4-part harmony sung to *Oo*
    Verse 2: Words sung in 4-part harmony
    Chorus: 4-part harmony sung to *Ah*
    Verse 3: Words sung in 4-part harmony
    Chorus: Unison voices
See also page 77 for glockenspiel part.

Music: French traditional melody
arranged © John Barnard/Jubilate Hymns †

Words: from the French
© Michael Perry/Jubilate Hymns †

44 Not in lordly state

Rhuddlan

Added descant for verse 4

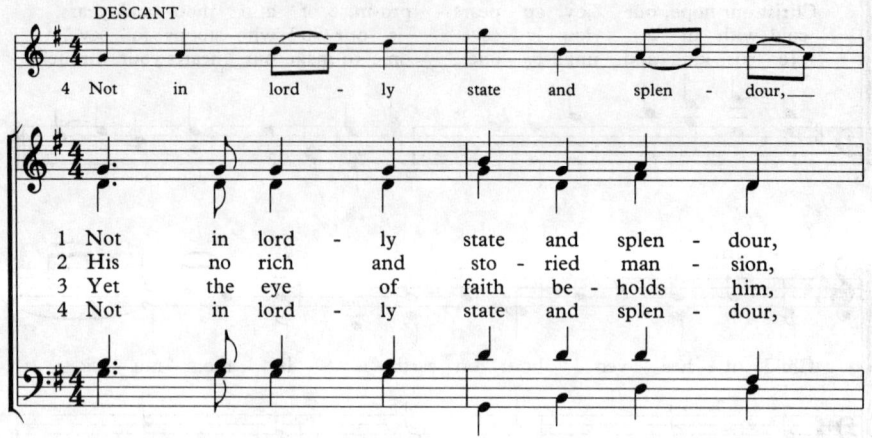

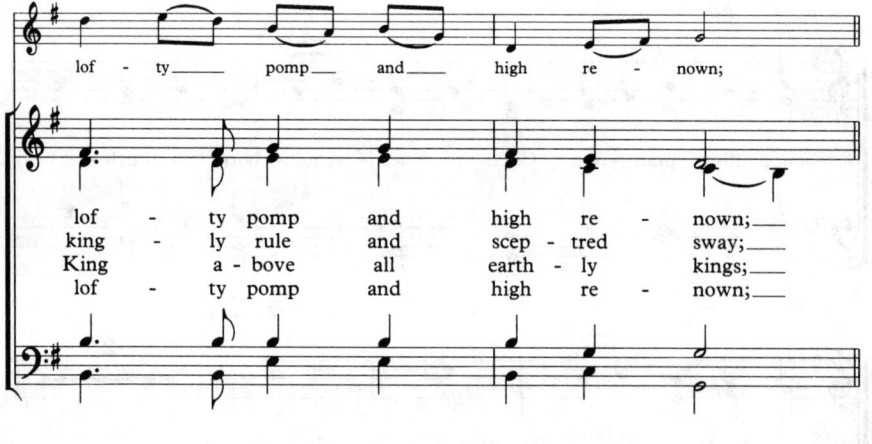

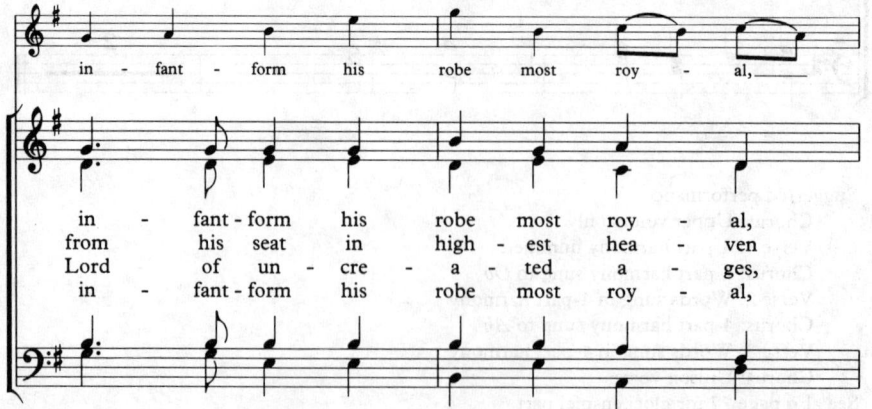

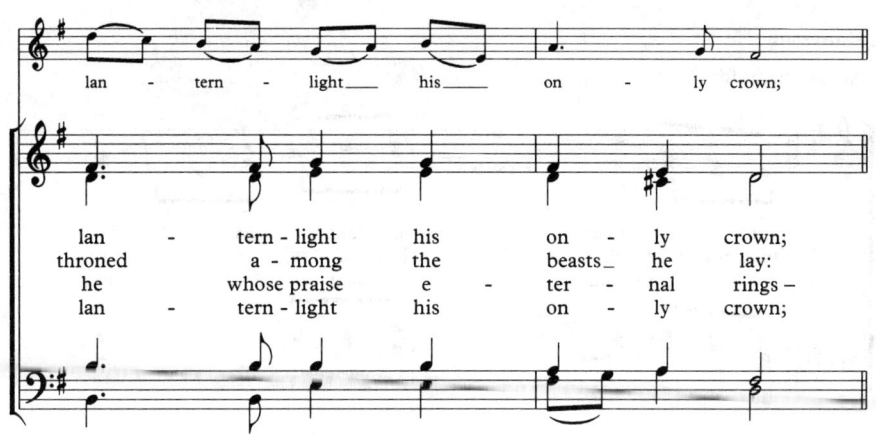
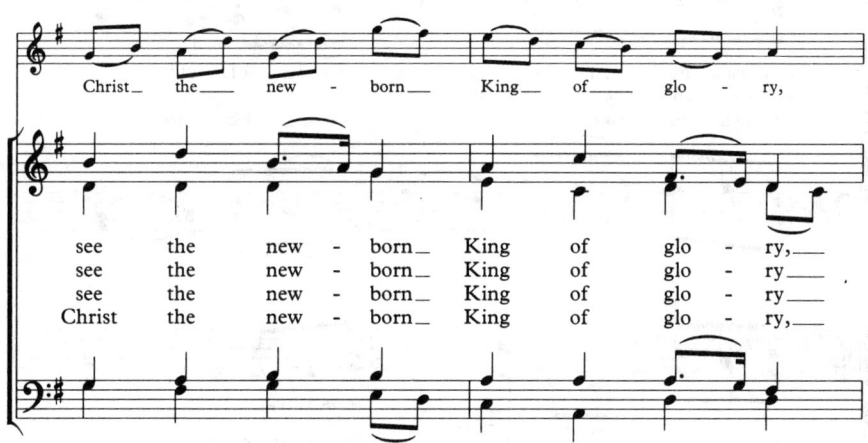
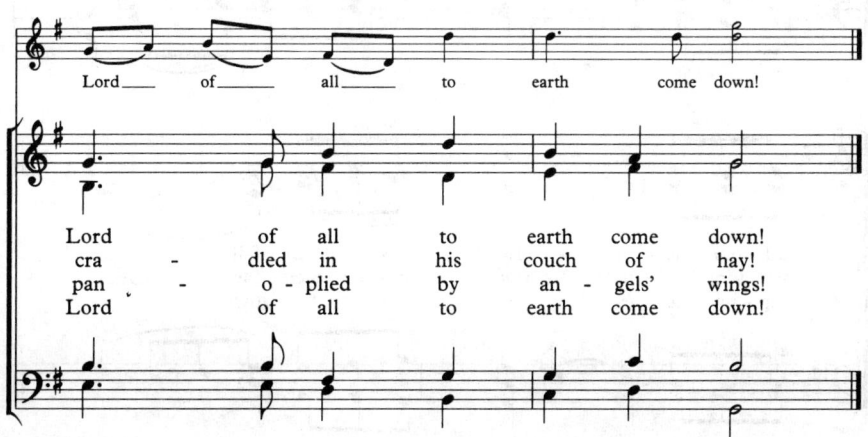

Music: Welsh traditional melody
from *Musical Relicks of the Welsh Bards* (1800)
descant © David Llewellyn Green

Words: © Timothy Dudley-Smith

45A Child in the manger

Bunessan

Arrangement for choir

1 Child in the manger, infant of Mary, outcast and stranger, Lord of all! child who inherits all our transgressions, all our demerits on him fall.

2 Once the most holy child of salvation gentle and lowly lived below: now as our glorious mighty redeemer, see him victorious over each foe.

3 Prophets foretold him, infant of wonder; angels behold him on his throne: worthy our saviour of all their praises; happy for ever are his own.

Music: Gaelic melody
arranged © David Llewellyn Green

Words: after M MacDonald (1789–1872)
L Macbean (1853–1931)

Mary had a baby, yes, Lord 49A

Mary had a baby

Introduction and arrangement for choir

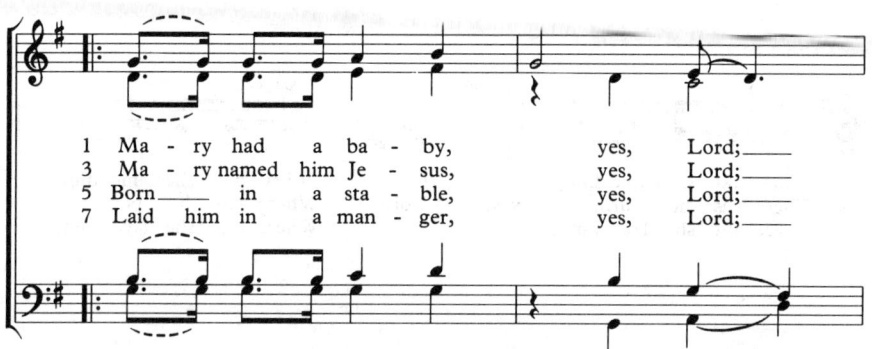

1 Mary had a baby, yes, Lord; Mary had a baby, yes, my Lord;
3 Mary named him Jesus, yes, Lord; Mary named him Jesus, yes, my Lord;
5 Born in a stable, yes, Lord; Born in a stable, yes, my Lord;
7 Laid him in a manger, yes, Lord; Laid him in a manger, yes, my Lord;

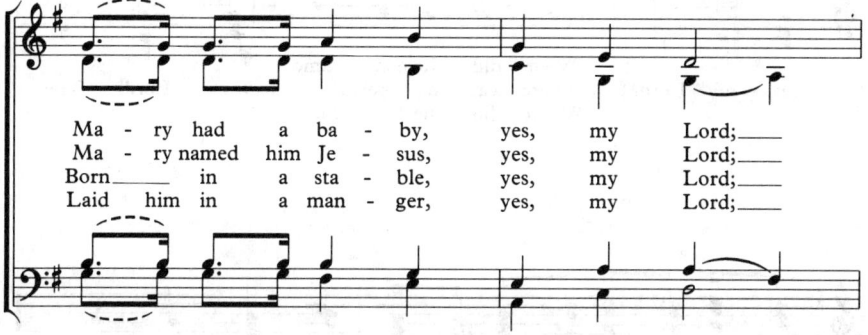

Mary had a baby, yes, Lord!
Mary named him Jesus, yes, Lord!
Born in a stable, yes, Lord!
Laid him in a manger, yes, Lord!

The

49A – Mary had a baby, yes, Lord

people keep a-com-ing but the train has gone! *Fine*
people come but the train has gone!

SOLO ... CHORUS ... SOLO
2 What did she name him,
4 Where was he born,— yes, Lord? What did she name him,
6 Where did she lay him, Where did she lay him,

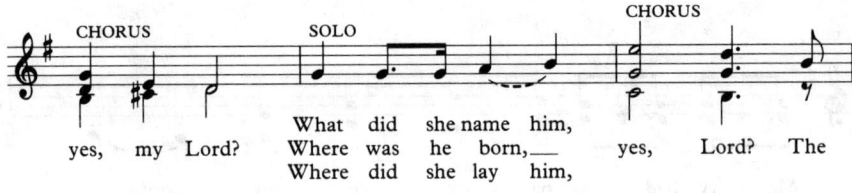
CHORUS ... SOLO ... CHORUS
What did she name him,
yes, my Lord? Where was he born,— yes, Lord? The
Where did she lay him,

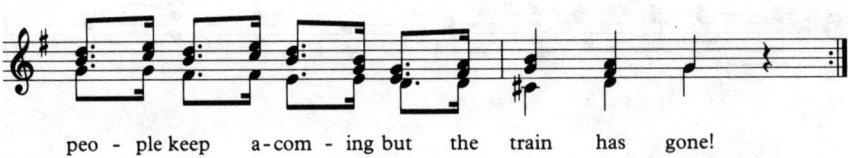
peo-ple keep a-com-ing but the train has gone!

Verses 2, 4 and 6 may be sung by a Soprano solo with Soprano 1, Soprano 2 and Alto chorus, or, an octave lower, by a Baritone solo with Tenor, Baritone and Bass chorus, or the verses may be shared between two such groups.

Music: West Indian traditional melody
arranged © David Iliff/Jubilate Hymns †

Words: West Indian carol
© in this version Word & Music/Jubilate Hymns †

Christ is born for us today 52A

Resonet in laudibus (ii)

Introduction and arrangement for choir

1 Christ is born for us to-day — rough the man-ger, soft the hay; all who will con-fess him may re-
2 Child of grace at Ma-ry's knee, he is born to set us free; he is born our hope to be, our
3 Christ-ians all, re-joice and sing with the com-ing of our King; let the bells of hea-ven ring to

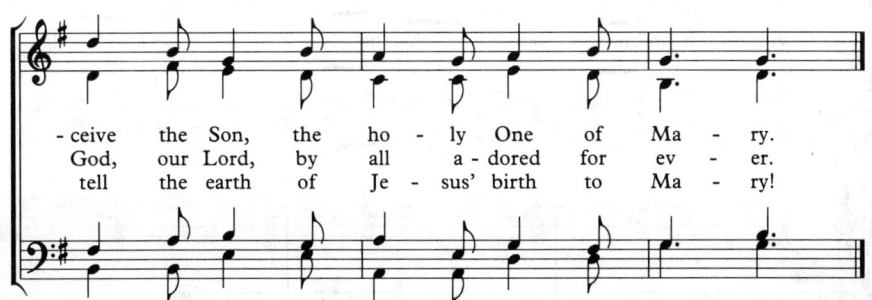

-ceive the Son, the ho-ly One of Ma-ry.
God, our Lord, by all a-dored for ev-er.
tell the earth of Je-sus' birth to Ma-ry!

Music: fourteenth-century German melody
arranged © David Iliff/Jubilate Hymns †

Words: J M Neale (1818–1866)
© in this version Word & Music/Jubilate Hymns †

61A I saw my love

O Waly Waly

Arrangement for Soprano solo, choir and organ

61A – I saw my love

Music: English traditional melody
arranged © Merion Powell

Words: © Paul Wigmore/Jubilate Hymns †

Glad music fills the Christmas sky 68

Deus tuorum militum

Added descant for verse 5

4 Let praise be true and love sincere,
  rejoice to greet the saviour's birth;
  let peace and honour fill the earth
  and mercy reign – for God is here!

5 Then lift your hearts and voices high,
  sing once again the Christmas song:
  for love and praise to Christ belong –
  in shouts of joy, and lullaby.

See also page 85 for trumpet part.

Music: Grenoble *Antiphoner* (1753)
arranged with descant © David Iliff/Jubilate Hymns †

Words: © Michael Perry/Jubilate Hymns †

85 Hear the skies around

Rajske strune zadonite

Music: Jugoslavian melody
arranged with descant © David Iliff/Jubilate Hymns †

Words: after the Jugoslavian carol
© Michael Perry/Jubilate Hymns †

89A All my heart this night rejoices

Bonn

Arrangement for choir and organ

Verses 2 and 3 overleaf

89A – All my heart this night rejoices

The part in the accompaniment marked Solo may be taken by a solo instrument.
The introduction for verses 1 and 4 may also be used for verses 2 and 3.

Music: J Ebeling (1637–1676)
arranged © Gareth Green

Words: after P Gerhardt (1607–1676)
C Winkworth (1827–1878)
© in this version Word & Music/Jubilate Hymns †

God to Adam came in Eden 97A

God is in Bethlehem

Arrangement for 4-part choir and organ

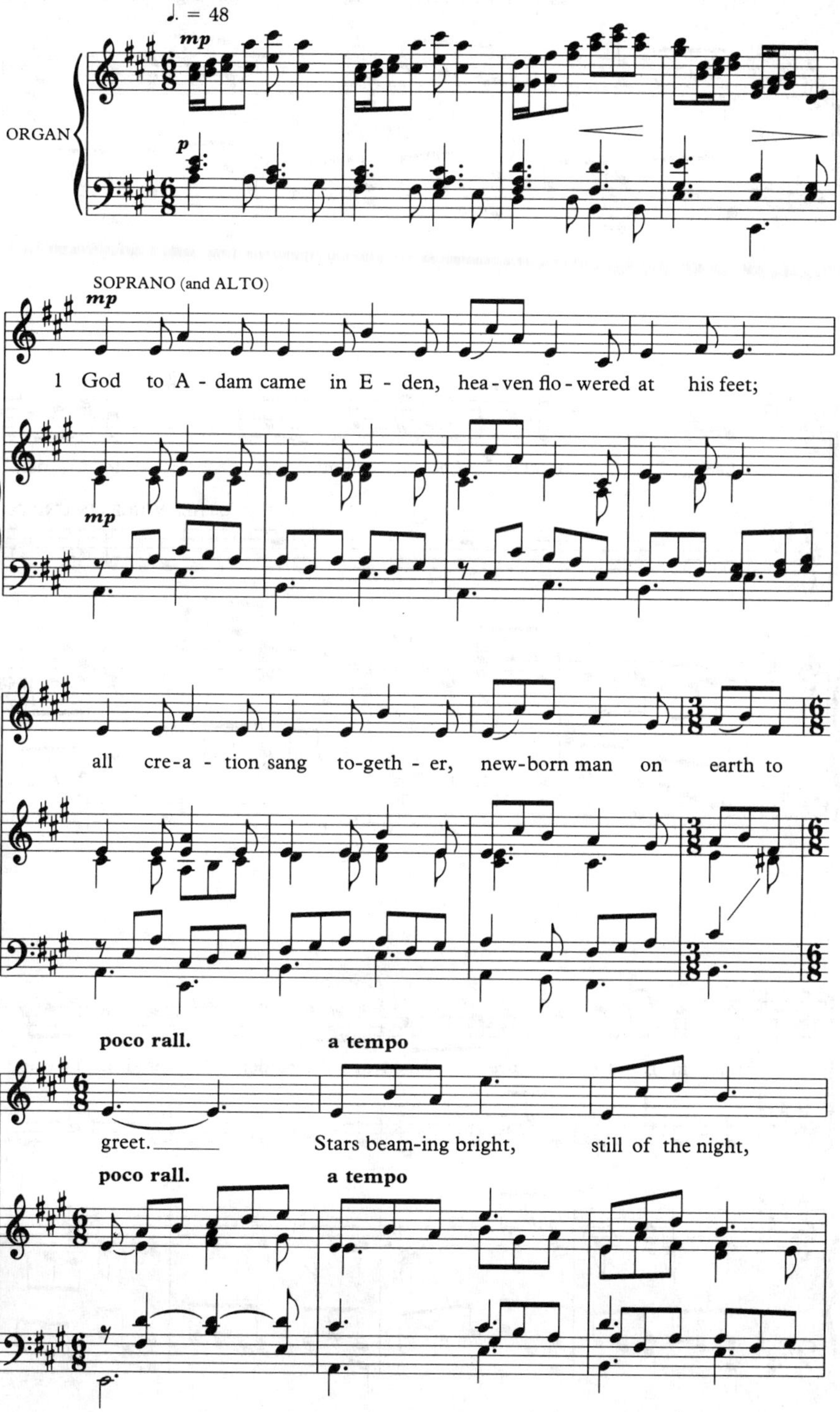

♩. = 48

1 God to A-dam came in E-den, hea-ven flo-wered at his feet; all cre-a-tion sang to-geth-er, new-born man on earth to greet. Stars beam-ing bright, still of the night,

97A – God to Adam came in Eden

97A – God to Adam came in Eden

97A – God to Adam came in Eden

The pitch is a semitone lower than the 2-part version in *Carols for Today* in order to accommodate men's voices. The versions are harmonically compatible and so the piano accompaniment for the 2-part arrangement may be used for this version or the organ accompaniment here may be used for the 2-part version.

Music: © John Barnard/Jubilate Hymns †   Words: © Paul Wigmore/Jubilate Hymns †

101 Come and sing the Christmas story

All through the night

Added arrangement for choir and/or organ with descant for verse 3

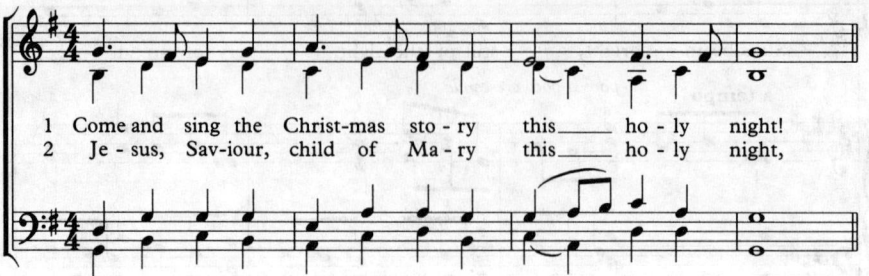

1 Come and sing the Christ-mas sto-ry this holy night!
2 Je-sus, Saviour, child of Ma-ry this holy night,

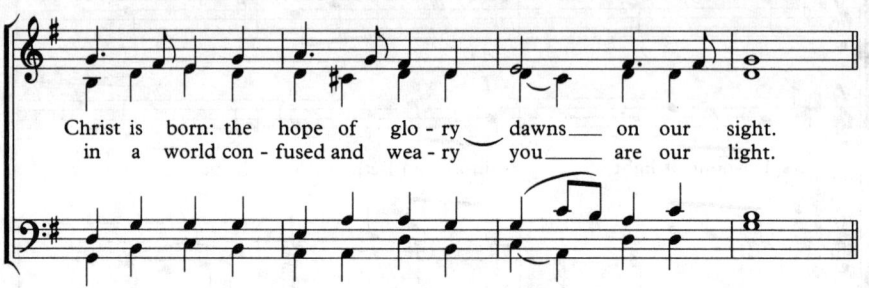

Christ is born: the hope of glo-ry dawns on our sight.
in a world con-fused and wea-ry you are our light.

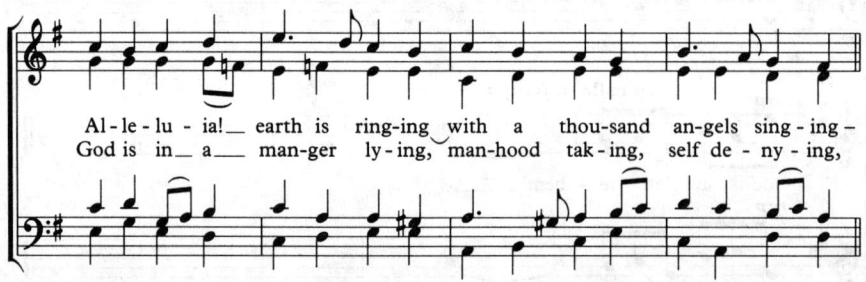

Al-le-lu-ia! earth is ring-ing with a thou-sand an-gels sing-ing—
God is in a man-ger ly-ing, man-hood tak-ing, self de-ny-ing,

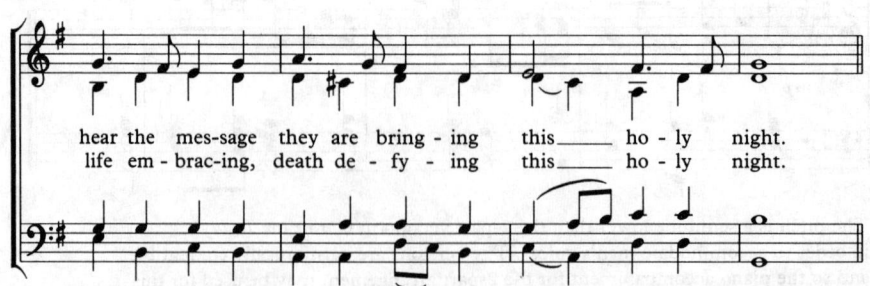

hear the mes-sage they are bring-ing this holy night.
life em-brac-ing, death de-fy-ing, this holy night.

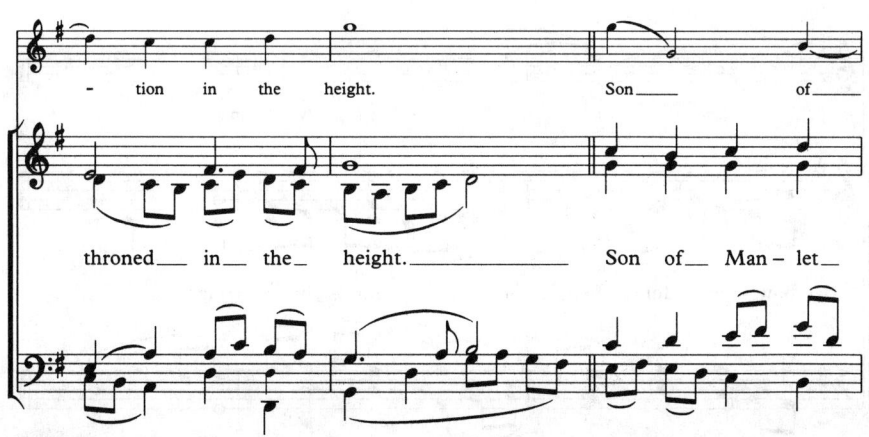

*or voices in unison with descant and organ accompaniment.

101 – Come and sing the Christmas story

Music: Welsh traditional melody
arranged © John Barnard/Jubilate Hymns †
verse 3 arranged with descant © 1989 David Llewellyn Green

Words: © Michael Perry/Jubilate Hymns †

See him lying on a bed of straw 110

Calypso Carol

Added arrangement for choir (SSATB) of the refrain

110 – See him lying on a bed of straw

The refrain may be sung by the upper voices alone.

Music: © Michael Perry/Jubilate Hymns †
arranged © David Iliff/Jubilate Hymns †

Words: © Michael Perry/Jubilate Hymns †

118 Christians, awake

Yorkshire

Added descant and accompaniment for verse 4

With them the joy - ful ti - dings first be - gan of
this day has God ful - filled the pro - mised word; this
In hu - man form their Shep - herd they dis - cern, and

Ma - ry's in - fant and our God made man.
day is born a sav - iour, Christ the Lord!'
to their flocks, still prais - ing God, re - turn.

DESCANT
4 O may we keep and pon - der in our mind

UNISON
4 O may we keep and pon - der in our mind

God's gra - cious love in sav - ing lost man - kind:

God's gra - cious love in sav - ing lost man - kind:

118 – Christians, awake

See also page 93 for trumpet part.

Music: J Wainwright (1723–1768)
arranged W H Monk (1823–1889)
verse 4 arranged with descant © John Barnard/Jubilate Hymns †

Words: J Byrom (1692–1763)
© in this version Word & Music/Jubilate Hymns †

Jesus, child of Mary

124A

Hayle

Arrangement for choir with descant

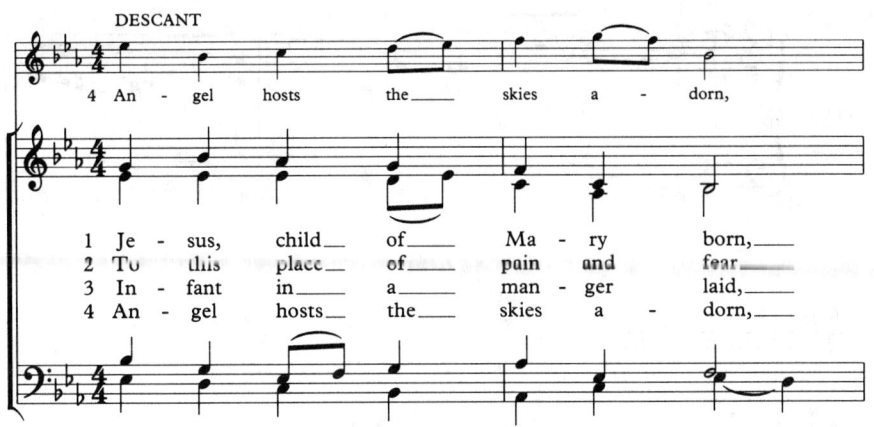

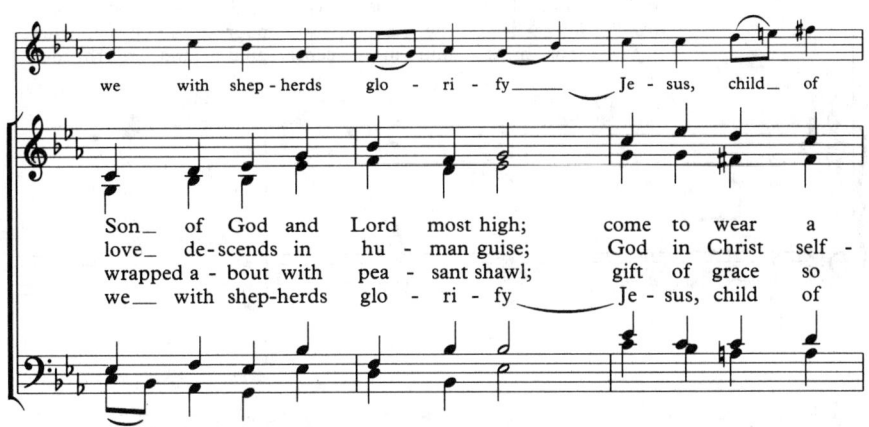

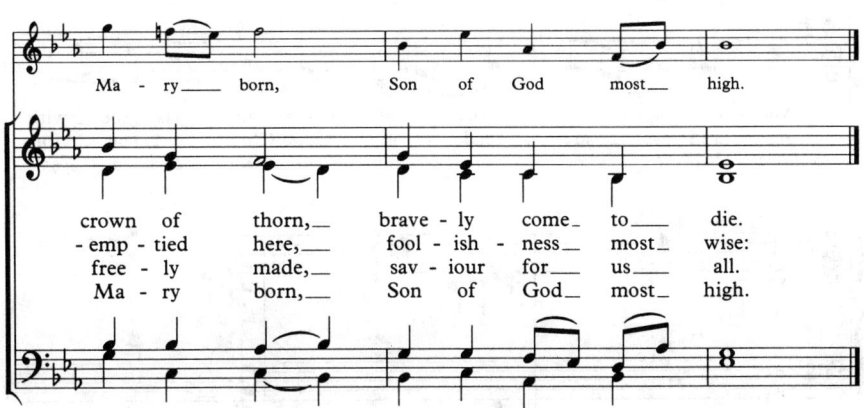

Music: © Michael Perry/Jubilate Hymns †
arranged with descant © David Iliff/Jubilate Hymns †

Words: © Michael Perry/Jubilate Hymns †

133A What Child is this

Greensleeves

Arrangement for unison voices (with descant) and piano

This arrangement may be used in conjunction with the
version in *Carols for Today* for one or more verses.

Music: English melody before 1642
arranged © Gareth Green

Words: W C Dix (1837–1898)
© in this version Word & Music/Jubilate Hymns †

143   Mary came with meekness

Noël nouvelet

Added introduction and fauxbourdon for verse 3

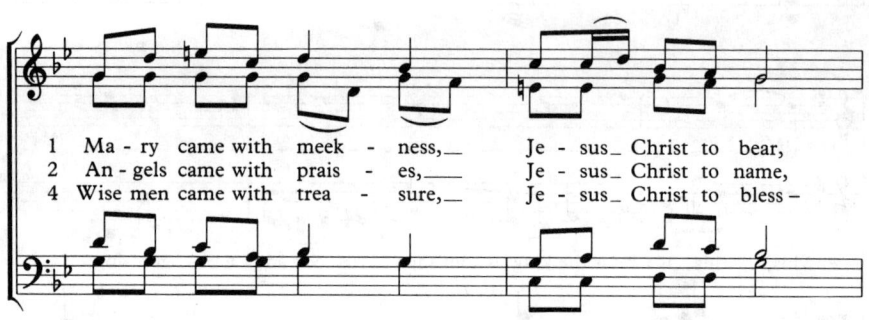

1 Ma - ry came with meek - ness,__ Je - sus Christ to bear,
2 An - gels came with prais - es,__ Je - sus Christ to name,
4 Wise men came with trea - sure,__ Je - sus Christ to bless —

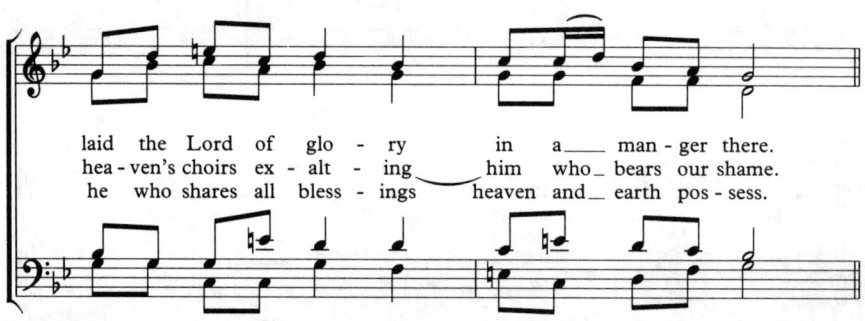

   laid the Lord of glo - ry in a__ man - ger there.
hea - ven's choirs ex - alt - ing him who__ bears our shame.
he who shares all bless - ings heaven and__ earth pos - sess.

We__ come re - joic - ing, Je - sus Christ to love:

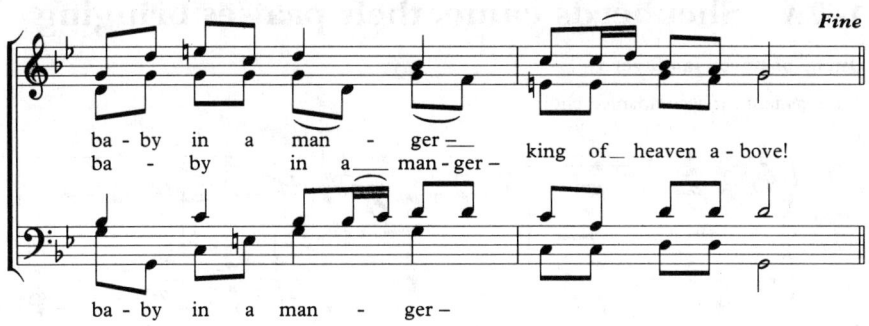

baby in a manger — king of heaven above!
baby in a manger —

baby in a manger —

Alternative version with melody in the tenor

Ah_____ Ah_____

3 Shep-herds came with tremb - ling, Je - sus Christ to see;

Ah_____ Ah_____

king who, at their bid - ding, would their shep-herd be.

We come re - joic - ing, Je - sus Christ to love:

baby in a manger — king of heaven above!

Music: French traditional melody
arranged © Tom Cunningham/Jubilate Hymns †

Words: © Paul Wigmore/Jubilate Hymns †

147A Shepherds came, their praises bringing

Quem pastores laudavere

Arrangement for accompanied choir

147A – Shepherds came, their praises bringing

Music: fourteenth-century German melody
arranged © Gareth Green

Words: from *Quem pastores laudavere* (fifteenth century)
G B Caird (1917–1984)
as revised by the author © Mrs V M Caird

The holly and the ivy 159

The holly and the ivy

Added introduction, interludes and arrangement for verse 6

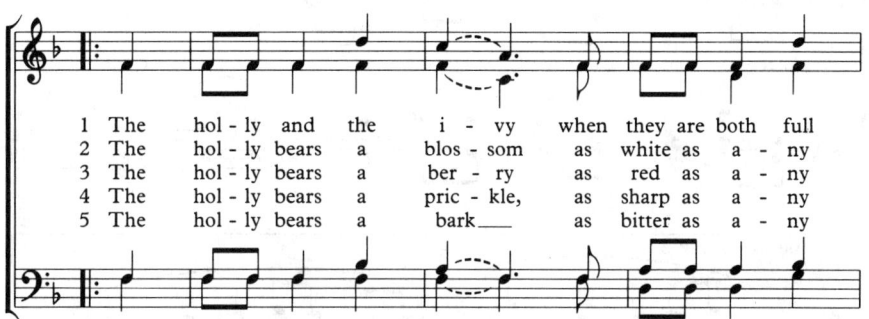

1 The hol-ly and the i-vy when they are both full grown — of all the trees that are in the wood, the hol-ly bears the crown.
2 The hol-ly bears a blos-som as white as a-ny flower; and Ma-ry bore sweet Je-sus Christ to be our true sav-iour.
3 The hol-ly bears a ber-ry as red as a-ny blood; and Ma-ry bore sweet Je-sus Christ to die for all our good.
4 The hol-ly bears a pric-kle, as sharp as a-ny thorn; and Ma-ry bore sweet Je-sus Christ to wear a cru-el crown.
5 The hol-ly bears a bark as bitter as a-ny gall; and Ma-ry bore sweet Je-sus Christ to suf-fer for us all.

Oh, the ris-ing of the sun and the

159 – The holly and the ivy

159 – The holly and the ivy

Suggested performance:
    Verse 1: Unison voices (accompanied)
    Verse 2: 4-part harmony (unaccompanied)
    Verse 3: upper voices (accompanied)
    Verse 4: lower voices (accompanied)
    Verse 5: 4-part harmony (unaccompanied)
    Verse 6: Unison voices (accompanied)

Music: English traditional melody
arranged © John Barnard/Jubilate Hymns †

Words: traditional © in this version
Word & Music/Jubilate Hymns †

Had he not loved us 166

Beacon Hill

Added descant for verse 3

1 Had he not loved us he had never come, yet is he lost in sorrow, sin and shame, the doors fast shut on our eternal home which now stand open — for he loved and came.

2 Had he not loved us he had never come; had he not come he need have never died nor won the victory of the vacant tomb, the awful triumph of the Crucified.

3 Had he not loved us he had never come; still were we lost in sorrow, sin and shame, the doors fast shut on our eternal home which now stand open — for he loved and came.

When the descant is sung all other voices sing the melody in unison throughout.

Music: © Peter White/Jubilate Hymns † Words: © Timothy Dudley-Smith

SECTION 2: INTRODUCTIONS

13 © Anthony Greening

19 © John Barnard/Jubilate Hymns †

May be used as an interlude between verses.

25 © John Barnard/Jubilate Hymns †

before verse 3

after verse 3   molto rall.

26

© Anthony Greening

May be used instead as an interlude between verses.

33

© John Barnard/Jubilate Hymns †

Introductions

50

© John Barnard/Jubilate Hymns †

51

© John Barnard/Jubilate Hymns †

54

© Anthony Greening

59

© David Iliff/Jubilate Hymns †

60

© Tom Cunningham/Jubilate Hymns †

See also flute part on page 77.

Introductions

66

© John Barnard/Jubilate Hymns †

Introduction: before verse 1

before verse 2

before verse 3

Man.

before verse 4

79

123

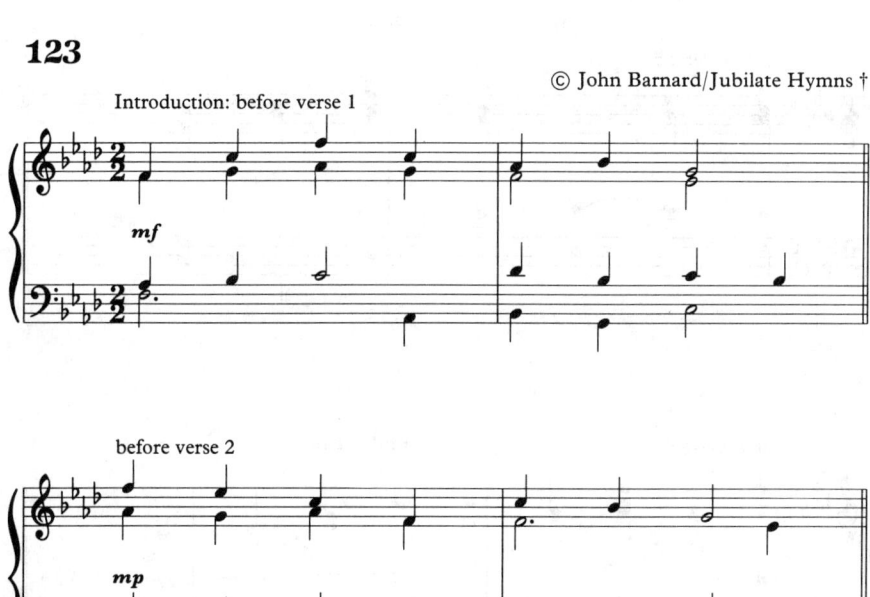

Introductions

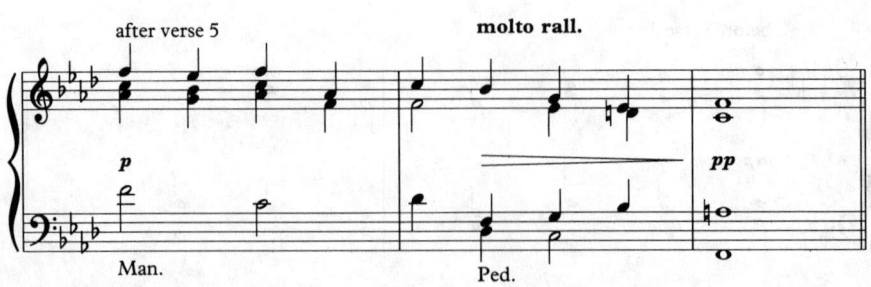

SECTION 3: INSTRUMENTAL PARTS

Permission is given for the reproduction by photocopy of items in this section on to single sheets for the convenience of performers.

Instrumental parts

See also keyboard introduction on page 73.

87

RECORDERS/FLUTES

© David Iliff/Jubilate Hymns †

Parts for B♭ Trumpet

In most cases the parts which follow are straight transcriptions of the tunes and descants from *Carols for Today*. Extra small-type notes are added for those who wish to play a more elaborate part. Care should be taken in the use of the small-type notes if the descant is to be sung as well as played.

Most of the parts may be played alternatively by B♭ clarinet.

1 © Merion Powell

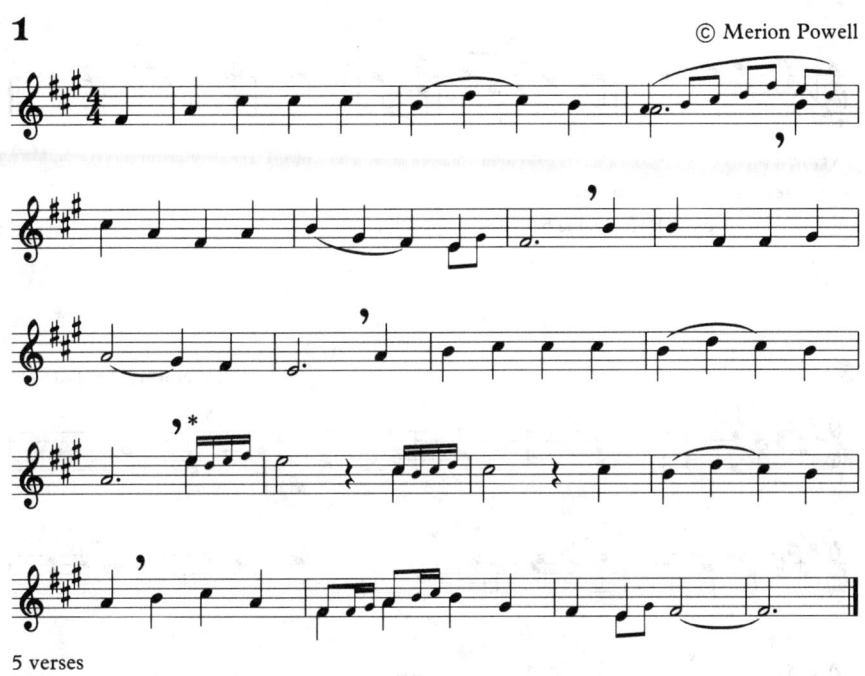

5 verses
Suggested use: play verses 1 and 5,
　　　　　　　play verses 2 and 3 from *

4 *Hymns and Sacred Poems* Dublin (1749)

Instrumental parts

© David Nield

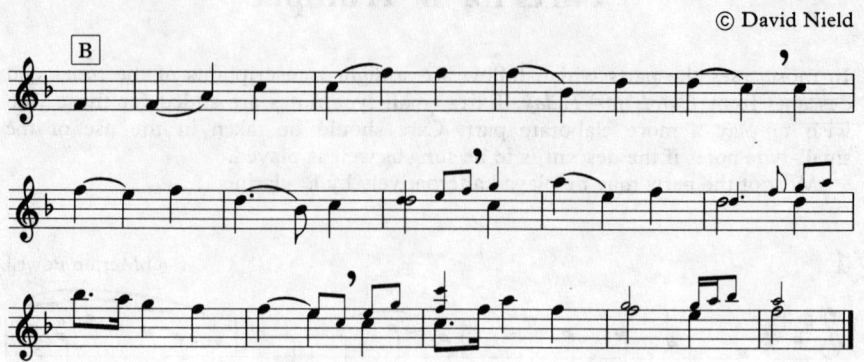

5 verses

Suggested use: play A for verse 4,
   play B for verse 5

5

M Praetorius (1571–1621)

© David Iliff/Jubilate Hymns †

5 verses

Suggested use: play A to * as introduction,
   play A for verse 4,
   play B for verse 5

9 / 172   J Leisentritt *Catholicum Hymnologium* (1584)

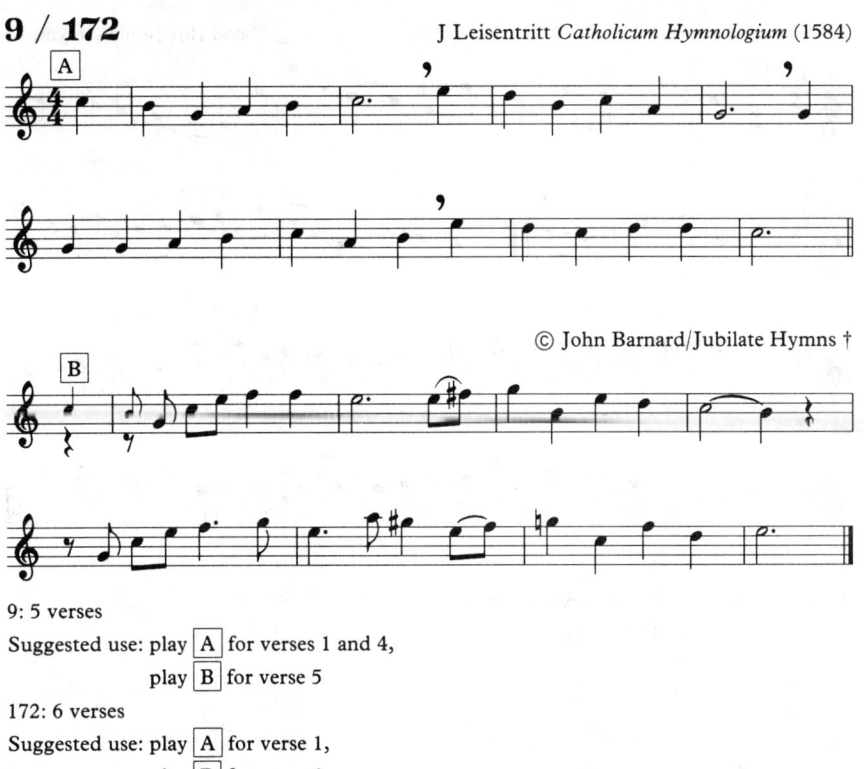

© John Barnard/Jubilate Hymns †

9: 5 verses

Suggested use: play A for verses 1 and 4,
               play B for verse 5

172: 6 verses

Suggested use: play A for verse 1,
               play B for verse 6

11   Eighteenth-century English melody

Instrumental parts

© David Iliff/Jubilate Hymns †

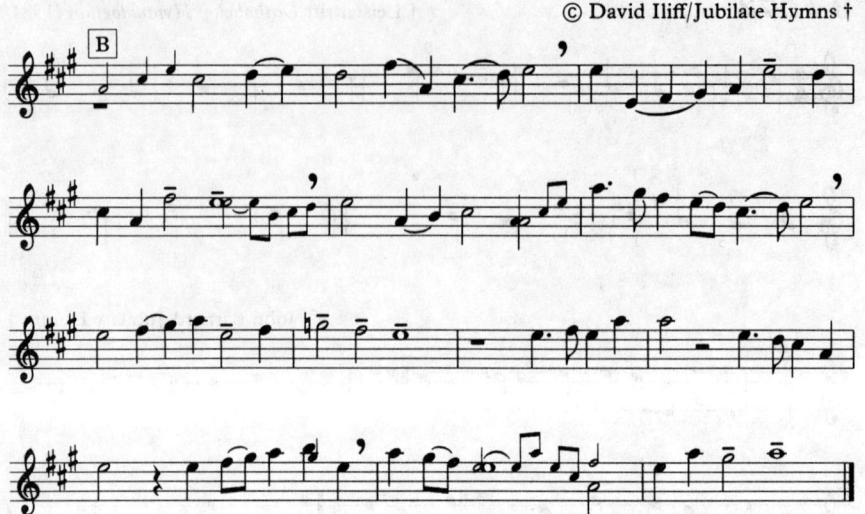

4 verses

Suggested use: play A for verses 1 and 3,
            play B for verse 4

12   W H Monk (1823–1889)

© John Barnard/Jubilate Hymns †

5 verses

Suggested use: play A for verses 1 and 2,
            play B for verse 5

14 Ravenscroft's *Psalter* (1621)

© David Iliff/Jubilate Hymns †

4 verses

Suggested use: play A for verses 1 and 2,
play B for verse 4

16 A Williams' *New Universal Psalmodist* (1770)

6 verses

Suggested use: play A for verses 1 and 5,
play B for verse 6

Instrumental parts

18   L Mason (1792–1872)

3 verses

Suggested use: play to * as introduction,
                  play verses 1 and 3

41   H J Gauntlett (1805–1876)

© Paul Edwards/Jubilate Hymns †

6 verses

Suggested use: play A for verse 5,
                  play B for verse 6

68 Grenoble *Antiphoner* (1753)

© David Iliff/Jubilate Hymns †

5 verses

Suggested use: play A for verse 4,
play B for verse 5

73 English traditional melody

5 verses

Suggested use: play verses 1 and 5,
play verses 3 and 4 from *

Instrumental parts

75 *Piae Cantiones (1582)*

© David Iliff/Jubilate Hymns †

5 verses

Suggested use: play A for verses 1 and 4,
   play B for verse 5

77

T Este's *Psalmes* (1592)

© John Barnard/Jubilate Hymns †

6 verses

Suggested use: play A for verses 1 and 5,
　　　　　　　play B for verse 6

84

F Mendelssohn (1809–1847)

Instrumental parts

© Christopher Robinson

3 verses

Suggested use: play A for verse 1,
      play B for verse 3

86   French melody

Alternative version for 2nd time from *

© John Barnard/Jubilate Hymns †

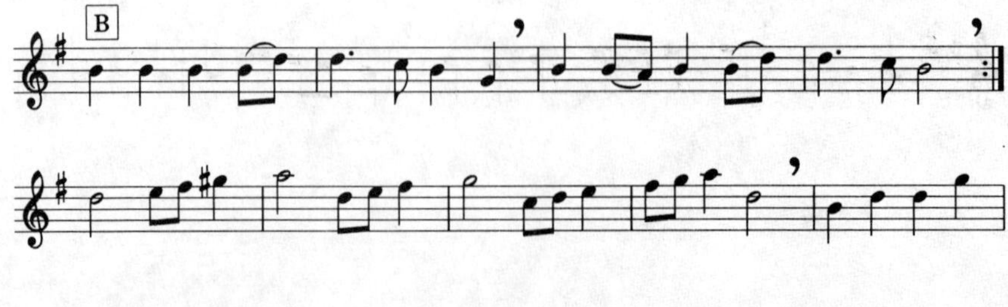

4 verses

Suggested use: play A for verse 1,
   play A from * for verse 2,
   play B for verse 4

92   A S Sullivan (1842–1900)

© Christopher Robinson

4 verses

Suggested use: play A for verse 1,
   play A from * for verse 3,
   play B for verse 4

Instrumental parts

100
English traditional melody

© David Iliff/Jubilate Hymns †

4 verses

Suggested use: play A for verses 1 and 3,
　　　　　　　play B for verse 4

102 / 103
J F Wade (1711–1786)

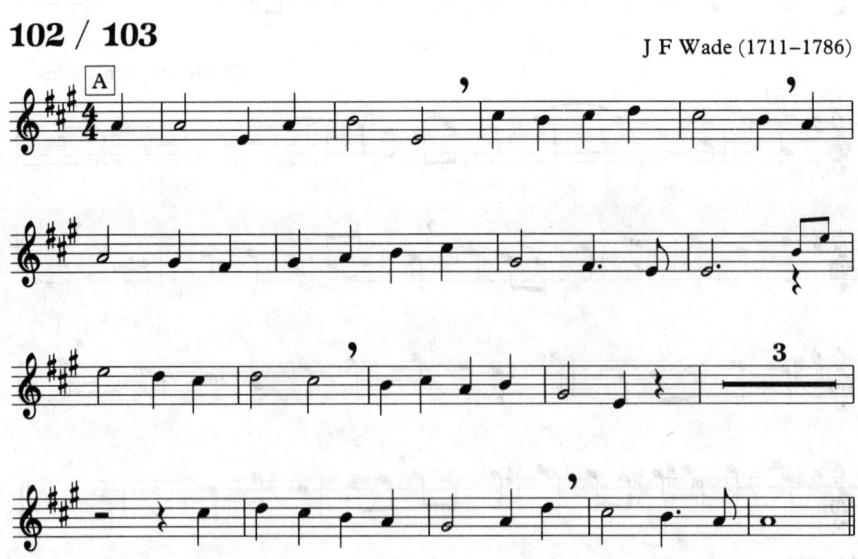

© Paul Edwards/Jubilate Hymns †

A should only be used for verse 1,
B may be used for any other verses as required,
C should only be used for the last verse

Instrumental parts

106 Welsh traditional melody

© David Iliff/Jubilate Hymns †

3 verses

Suggested use: play A for verse 1,
                play B for verse 3

107 © Paul Edwards/Jubilate Hymns †

4 verses

Suggested use: play A for verse 1,
                play B for verse 4

118   J Wainwright (1723–1768)

© John Barnard/Jubilate Hymns †

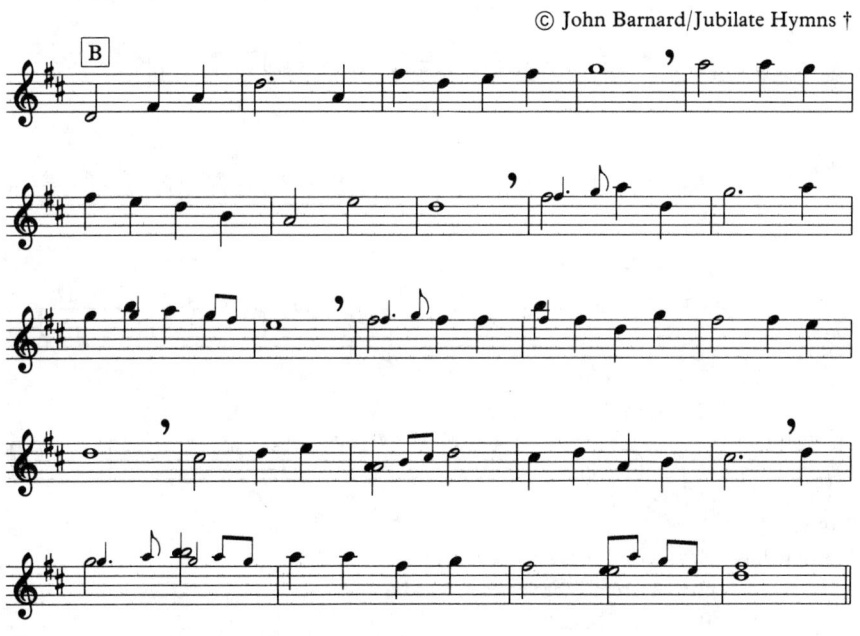

4 verses

Suggested use: play A for verses 1 and 3,
                play B for verse 4

Note: version B is compatible only with the accompaniment for verse 4 in this book.

Instrumental parts

120 English traditional melody

© Christopher Robinson

7 verses

Suggested use: play A for verses 1 and 5,
  play A from * for verses 2, 3 and 4,
  play B for verse 7

128 *Piae Cantiones* (1582)

4 verses

Suggested use: play verses 1 and 4

130 *Piae Cantiones* (1582)

© David Iliff/Jubilate Hymns †

5 verses

Suggested use: play A to * as introduction,
              play A for verses 1 and 2,
              play B for verse 5

Instrumental parts

5 verses

Suggested use: play A for verses 1 and 3,
     play B for verse 5

© Merion Powell

4 verses

Suggested use: play A for verse 1,
play A from * for verses 2 and 3,
play B for verse 4

146 C Kocher (1786–1872)

© John Barnard/Jubilate Hymns †

5 verses

Suggested use: play A for verse 1,
play B for verse 5

160 *Musikalisches Handbuch* (1690)

© John Barnard/Jubilate Hymns †

5 verses

Suggested use: play A for verses 1 and 4,
play B for verse 5

172 See 9 on page 81

176 Fifteenth-century English melody

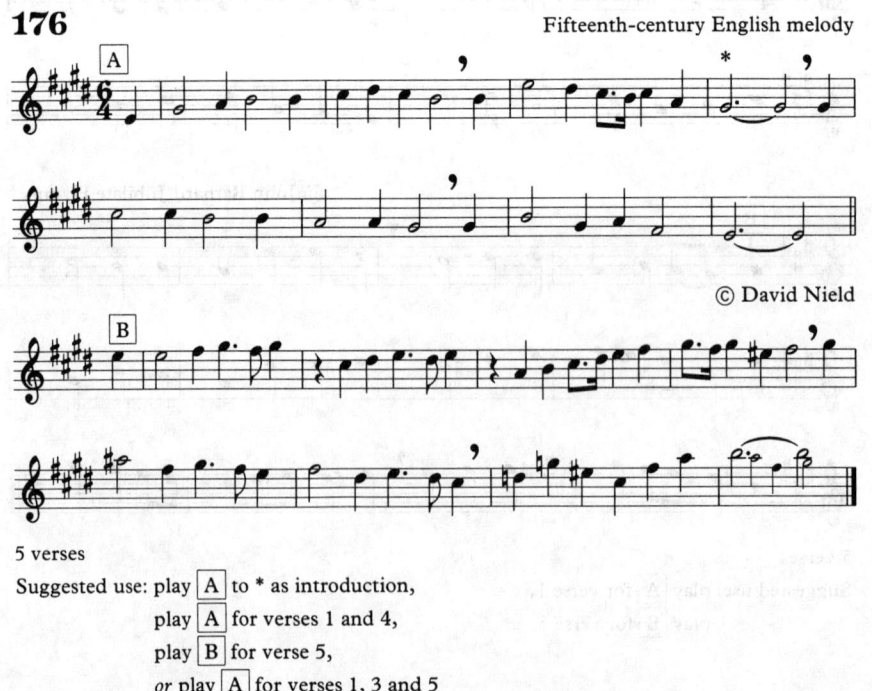

© David Nield

5 verses

Suggested use: play A to * as introduction,
play A for verses 1 and 4,
play B for verse 5,
or play A for verses 1, 3 and 5

LEGAL INFORMATION

Those seeking to reprint works in this book which are the property of Jubilate Hymns or associated authors and composers, including items by Word & Music, may write to The Copyright Manager, Jubilate Hymns Ltd., 61 Chessel Avenue, Southampton SO2 4DY (telephone 0703 630038). In the United States these same copyrights, along with those of Timothy Dudley-Smith, are administered by Hope Publishing Company, Carol Stream, Illinois 60188, USA. Addresses of other copyright holders can also be supplied.

A number of church music publishers have uniform concessions and rates. Details are available from The Copyright Manager, Jubilate Hymns Ltd.

Most of these publishers also combine to offer a licensing scheme for limited term reproduction of words. Where this is felt to be an advantage, application should be made to the Christian Music Association at Glyndley Manor, Stone Cross, Pevensey, East Sussex BN24 5BS (telephone 0323 440440).

Recording and Broadcasting
Jubilate Hymns with their associated authors and composers, and Word & Music, are members of the Mechanical Copyright Protection and Performing Rights Societies. Appropriate application should be made to these bodies as follows: The Mechanical Copyright Protection Society, Elgar House, 41 Streatham High Road, London SW16 1ER (telephone 081 769 4400); The Performing Rights Society, 29–33 Berners Street, London W1P 4AA (telephone 071 580 5544).

FIRST LINES, TITLES AND ORIGINAL SOURCES INDEX

Titles printed in bold type indicate items for which additional material is printed in this book.

Titles printed in ordinary type appear only in the main volume, *Carols for Today*.

Column 1 (CFT) Numbers in this column apply to both books. Items with the suffix A (e.g. 43A) are settings in the Supplement which are not compatible with the music at the corresponding number in *Carols for Today*.

Column 2 (Supp) These are *page* numbers in the Supplement, given because items are not arranged in numerical order.

Column 3 (Cong) Indicates suitability of the item for congregational/audience use.

Column 4 (Anth) Indicates suitability of the item for choir use as an anthem.

Column 5 (Unis) The setting may be sung by unison voices with accompaniment.

Column 6 (SATB) The setting is in harmony and may be sung *a cappella* (unaccompanied).

Column 7 (Instr) An instrumental part is provided in Section 3 of this Supplement.

○ The item appears in *Carols for Today* only.

◐ The item appears in *Carols for Today* and additional material appears in the Supplement.

● Material appears in the Supplement which may be used independently of the main book.

	CFT	Supp	Cong	Anth	Unis	SATB	Instr
A child is born in Bethlehem (A child is born)	126		○		○		
A child is born in Bethlehem (Sing nowell)	127		○	○		○	
A child this day is born	117		○			○	
A great and mighty wonder	95		○	○		○	
A little child there is y-born –							
see Descend from heaven, you angels bright							
A song was heard at Christmas	178			○	○	○	
A stable lamp is lighted	36			○	○	○	
A tender shoot has started	24			○			○
A virgin most holy	33	71	◐	◐			◐
A virgin most pure –							
see A virgin most holy							
A virgin unspotted –							
see A virgin most holy							

Title	CFT	Supp	Cong	Anth	Unis	SATB	Instr
Adeste fideles laeti triumphantes – *see* O come, all ye faithful							
All my heart this night rejoices (All my heart)	90		○		○		
All my heart this night rejoices (Bonn)	89	38	◐	◐		◐	
All through the night – *see* Come and sing the Christmas story							
Angels from the realms of glory	86	88	○			○	●
Angelus ad virginem – *see* Gabriel the angel came							
As Joseph was awaking (Cherry Tree Carol)	30		○	○		○	
As Joseph was awaking (Joseph)	31			○		○	
As with gladness men of old	146	97	○			○	●
Away in a manger	57		○	○		○	
Before the heaven and earth (Munden)	171		○		○		
Before the heaven and earth (Narenza)	172	81	○			○	●
Behold a little tender babe – *see* Come see a little tender babe							
Behold, the great Creator makes (Kilmarnock)	175		○			○	
Behold, the great Creator makes (This endris nyght)	176	98	○	○		○	●
Bellman's Carol – *see* When came in flesh the incarnate Word							
Besançon Carol – *see* Mary, ride on to David's town *and* People, look east							
Bethlehem, we come to bring	113		○	○	○		
Bethlehem, what greater city	134	96	○			○	●
Bow down, you stars	23		○	○		○	
Bright mystical starlight	137			○		○	
Brightest and best	140		○			○	
Calypso Carol – *see* See him lying on a bed of straw							
Cherry Tree Carol – *see* As Joseph was awaking							
Child in a stable	35			○		○	
Child in the manger	45	26	○	●	○	●	
Child of heaven born on earth	43	22,77		◐	○	●	●
Child of mine, the Virgin sings	158			○		○	
Child of the stable's secret birth (Morwenstow)	46		○	○	○	○	
Child of the stable's secret birth (Secret Birth)	47		○	○		○	
Child, when Herod wakes	153		○	○	○		
Christ is born for us today	52	29	○	●	○	●	
Christ is born within a stable	114		○	○		○	○
Christ is the Truth sent from above	19	70		◐		○	
Christians, awake	118	54,93	◐			◐	●
Christians, make a joyful sound	74			○		○	
Christmas for God's holy people	122		○	○	○		
Come and hear the joyful singing	106	92	○	○		○	●
Come and sing the Christmas story	101	48	○	●		○	
Come, O long-expected Jesus	2	6	◐			◐	
Come, see a little tender babe (Newtown Linford)	37	18		◐	○	●	
Come, see a little tender babe (Peak Hill)	38			○		○	
Come, thou long-expected Jesus – *see* Come, O long-expected Jesus							

	CFT	Supp	Cong	Anth	Unis	SATB	Instr
Come, thou redeemer of the earth –							
see O come, our world's Redeemer, come							
Come to Bethlehem and see the new-born king	71				O	O	O
Conditor alme siderum –							
see Creator of the stars of light							
Corde natus ex Parentis –							
see God of God, the uncreated							
Coventry Carol –							
see Hush, do not cry							
Creator of the stars of light	3				O	O	O
Dans cette étable –							
see Child in a stable							
Deck the hall with boughs of holly –							
see Come and hear the joyful singing							
Descend from heaven, you angels bright	66	74			◐		O
Ding-dong ding –							
see Wake then, Christian, come and listen							
Ding-dong! Merrily on high	99		O	O		O	
Donkey and ox around his bed	50	72	◐			◐	
Donkey and ox around his bed	51	73	◐				O
Dormi Jesu! Mater ridet –							
see Sleep, Lord Jesus!							
Down from the height (Purpose)	173			O		O	
Down from the height (Slane)	174			O		O	
Earth has many a noble city –							
see Bethlehem, what greater city							
Echo Carol –							
see From highest heaven where praises ring							
Entre le boeuf et l'âne gris –							
see Donkey and ox around his bed							
Es ist ein' Ros' –							
see A great and mighty wonder							
Es wird scho glei dumpa –							
see The daylight is fading							
Et barn er født i Betlehem –							
see A child is born in Bethlehem							
Every star shall sing a carol –							
see Christmas for God's holy people							
Faithful vigil ended	154			O		O	
Fragrance –							
see Word of the Father everlasting							
Freut euch und singt –							
see Rejoice and sing							
Fröhlich soll mein Herze springen –							
see All my heart this night rejoices							
From east to west, from shore to shore	91		O			O	
From highest heaven where praises ring	79	77		◐		O	
Gabriel's Message –							
see The angel Gabriel from heaven came							
Gabriel the angel came	25			◐		O	
Gallery Carol –							
see Rejoice and be merry							
Gaudete, gaudete, Christus est natus –							
see Rejoice with heart and voice							

Title	CFT	Supp	Cong	Anth	Unis	SATB	Instr
Geborn ist uns ein Kindelein – *see* Travellers all to Bethlehem							
Girls and boys, leave your toys	115		○	○	○		
Glad music fills the Christmas sky	68	35,85	○			◐	●
Go, tell it on the mountain	78			○		○	
God of God, the uncreated	75	86	○		○		●
God rest you merry, gentlemen	120	94	○			○	●
God to Adam came in Eden	97	41		●	○		
Good Christian men, rejoice – *see* Good Christians all, rejoice							
Good Christian people, rise and sing	98		○	○		○	
Good Christians all, rejoice	70		○	○		○	
Good King Wenceslas looked out	177		○			○	
Had he not loved us	166	69		◐		◐	
Hajej, nynej – *see* Jesus, saviour, holy child							
Hark, a thrilling voice is sounding – *see* Hark! a trumpet call is sounding							
Hark! a trumpet call is sounding	12	82	○			○	●
Hark! do you hear how the angel voices sing	144			○	○		
Hark the glad sound	14	83	○			○	●
Hark! the herald angels sing	84	87	○			○	●
He comes to us as one unknown	167		○	○	○		
Hear the skies around	85		○	◐	○		
He is born, the king divine – *see* Child of heaven born on earth							
Holy child, how still you lie (Holy child)	56		○	○	○		
Holy child, how still you lie (Ruxley)	55		○	○		○	
Holy, joyful dawn of Christmas	94		○	○		○	
How brightly gleams the morning star	135			○		○	
How joyful is the song	179		○			○	
Hush, do not cry, my little tiny child	152			○		○	
I heard a mother tenderly sing	67			○		○	
I himmelen, i himmelen – *see* The star of heaven foretells							
I saw a fair maiden sitten and sing – *see* I heard a mother tenderly sing							
I saw my love by lantern light	61	30	○	●		○	
I saw three ships – *see* When God from heaven to earth came down							
I see your crib	54	73		◐		○	
I wonder as I wander	169			○		○	
Ihr Kinderlein kommet – *see* O come, all you children							
Il est né le divin enfant – *see* Child of heaven born on earth							
Il s'en va loin de la terre – *see* Jesus, child of gentle Mary							
In dieser armen Krippe liegt – *see* Within this humble manger lies							
In dulci jubilo – *see* Good Christians all, rejoice							
In the bleak mid-winter	42		○	○		○	
Infant holy, infant lowly	83		○	○		○	

Title	CFT	Supp	Cong	Anth	Unis	SATB	Instr
Instantis adventum Dei – *see* We hail the approaching God							
It came upon the midnight clear	92	89	O			O	●
Jesus, child of gentle Mary	151			O		O	
Jesus, child of Mary	124	57	O	●		◐	
Jesus Christ the Lord is born	130	95	O			O	●
Jesus, good above all other	181			O		O	
Jesus – hope of every nation	17			O		O	
Jesus noster, Jesus bonus – *see* Jesus, good above all other							
Jesus, saviour, holy child	64		O	O		O	
Jesus the saviour comes	15			O		O	
Jesus, you are welcome	145			O		O	
Jezus malusienki – *see* Such a night in Bethlehem							
Jordans orus praeria – *see* On Jordan's bank the Baptist's cry							
Joseph was an old man – *see* As Joseph was awaking							
Joy to the world! The Lord has come	18	84	O	O		O	●
Joy to the world! The Lord has come	18A	8		●			
Lift up your heads, you mighty gates	6		O		O		
Lift your heart and raise your voice	107	92	O	O	O		●
Little children, wake and listen	112		O	O		O	
Little Jesus, sweetly sleep – *see* Jesus, saviour, holy child							
Lo, he comes with clouds descending	11	81	O			O	●
Lord, now let your servant (Caswall)	157		O			O	
Lord, now let your servant (North Coates)	156		O			O	
Love came down at Christmas (Gartan)	164		O			O	
Love came down at Christmas (Hermitage)	165		O	O	O		
Love is come again – *see* Mary came with meekness							
Lullay, lullay, thou little tiny child – *see* Hush, do not cry							
Lullay my liking – *see* I heard a mother tenderly sing							
Magnificat – *see* My soul proclaims the greatness of the Lord *and* Now sing my soul, 'How great the Lord!'							
Mary came with meekness	143	60		◐		◐	
Mary had a baby – sweet lamb	48			O		O	
Mary had a baby, yes, Lord	49	27	O	●	O	●	
Mary, ride on to David's town	34			O	O	O	
Mega kai paradoxa thauma – *see* A great and mighty wonder							
My soul proclaims the greatness of the Lord	28			O	O	O	
Nesem vam noviny – *see* Softly, a shepherd is singing							
No frightened shepherds now	184			O	O	O	
No small wonder – *see* Small wonder the star							
Noël nouvelet – *see* Mary came with meekness							

	CFT	Supp	Cong	Anth	Unis	SATB	Instr
Nos Galan –							
see Come and hear the joyful singing							
Not in lordly state and splendour	44	24	○			◐	
Now sing my soul, 'How great the Lord!'	29		○			○	
Now the green blade riseth –							
see Mary came with meekness							
Now the holly bears a berry –							
see When the angel came to Mary							
Nu zijt wellekome –							
see Jesus, you are welcome							
Nunc dimittis –							
see Faithful vigil ended							
and Jesus – hope of every nation							
and Lord, now let your servant							
O Babe divine, to you we sing	180			○		○	
O come, all ye faithful	102	90	○			○	●
O come, all ye faithful (long version)	103	90	○			○	●
O come all you children	104		○			○	
O come all you children	105			○			
O come, O come, Emmanuel	1	79	○		○		●
O come, O come, Emmanuel	1A	2		●		●	
O come, our world's Redeemer, come	5	7,80	○	○		◐	●
O du fröhliche –							
see Holy, joyful dawn of Christmas							
O Jesus my Lord, how sweetly you lie	65			○		○	
O Jesulein süss –							
see O Jesus my Lord, how sweetly you lie							
O leave your sheep	109			○		○	
O little one sweet –							
see O Jesus my Lord, how sweetly you lie							
O little town of Bethlehem (Christmas Carol)	40		○			○	
O little town of Bethlehem (Forest Green)	39		○			○	
O Prince of peace	93		○	○		○	
O slumber, heaven-born treasure	59	73		◐		○	
O sola magnarium urbium –							
see Bethlehem, what greater city							
O solis ortus cardine –							
see From east to west, from shore to shore							
O worship the Lord in the beauty of holiness	150		○			○	
Of the Father's love begotten –							
see God of God, the uncreated							
On Christmas night all Christians sing –							
see Good Christian people, rise and sing							
On Jordan's bank the Baptist's cry	160	98	○			○	●
Once in royal David's city	41	84	○			○	●
Past three a clock –							
see Ring out the bells							
Patapan –							
see Bethlehem, we come to bring							
People, look east	13	70		◐		○	
Personent hodie –							
see Shout aloud, girls and boys							
Quelle est cette odeur –							
see Word of the Father everlasting							

	CFT	Supp	Cong	Anth	Unis	SATB	Instr
Quem pastores laudavere –							
see Jesus, good above all other							
and Shepherds came, their praises bringing							
Quittez pasteurs –							
see O leave your sheep							
Rajske strune zadonite –							
see Hear the skies around							
Rejoice and be merry	141		○	○		○	
Rejoice and sing	170			○		○	
Rejoice with heart and voice	72			○		○	
Resonet in laudibus –							
see Christ is born for us today							
and Christians, make a joyful sound							
Ring out the bells	129		○	○		○	
Rise up, shepherd, and follow –							
see There's a Saviour to see							
Sans Day Carol –							
see When the angel came to Mary							
Schlaf wohl –							
see O slumber, heaven-born treasure							
See, amid the winter snow	119		○		○	○	
See him lying on a bed of straw	110	51	○	●	○		
See him lying on a bed of straw	111		○		○		
Shepherd-boy, tell me, why are you singing	116			○		○	
Shepherds came, their praises bringing	147	62	○	●		○	
Shepherd's Cradle Song –							
see O slumber, heaven-born treasure							
Shepherds' Farewell –							
see Jesus, child of gentle Mary							
Shepherds in the fields abiding –							
see Angels from the realms of glory							
Shepherds left their flocks a-straying –							
see Shepherds came, their praises bringing							
Shepherds, O hark ye, glad tidings we bring –							
see Softly, a shepherd is singing							
Shout aloud, girls and boys	128		○	○	○		
Silent night! holy night	80		○			○	
Sing lullaby! lullaby baby	58			○		○	
Sing, oh sing, this happy morn	73	85	○			○	●
Sleep, Lord Jesus!	60	73, 77		●		○	●
Sleepers wake! –							
see Wake, O wake, and sleep no longer							
Small wonder the star	148		○	○		○	
Small wonder the star	149			○			
Softly, a shepherd is singing	87	78		○		○	●
Softly, a shepherd is singing	88		○	○		○	
Song of Christ's glory							
see Before the heaven and earth							
and Down from the height							
Song of Mary –							
see My soul proclaims the greatness of the Lord							
and Now sing my soul, 'How great the Lord!'							

Title	CFT	Supp	Cong	Anth	Unis	SATB	Instr
Song of Simeon –							
see Faithful vigil ended							
and Jesus – hope of every nation							
and Lord, now let your servant							
Songs of thankfulness and praise (St Edmund)	161		○			○	
Songs of thankfulness and praise (St George's, Windsor)	162		○			○	
Stars of heaven, clear and bright	123	75	○	◐		○	
Still, still, still	96			○		○	
Stille Nacht! heilige Nacht –							
see Silent night! holy night							
Stranger in Bethlehem –							
see To Bethlehem the strangers came							
Such a night in Bethlehem	125			○	○		
Susanni –							
see Descend from heaven, you angels bright							
Sussex Carol –							
see Good Christian people, rise and sing							
Take God's good news to saddened hearts	8		○			○	
Thank you, God, for Mary's child	182			○	○	○	
The advent of our King –							
see We hail the approaching God							
The angel Gabriel from heaven came	27			○		○	
The Angels and the Shepherds –							
see Softly, a shepherd is singing							
The darkness turns to dawn (Saigon)	21	16	○	●	○	●	
The darkness turns to dawn (Sandys)	22		○			○	
The daylight is fading	62		○	○		○	
The daylight is fading	63			○	○		
The first nowell	142	96	○			○	●
The God we seek	168			○		○	
The holly and the ivy	159	65	○	●		○	
The Lord of life and glory	155			○	○	○	
The Lord will come and not be slow	7		○			○	
The moon shines bright –							
see When came in flesh the incarnate Word							
The people who in darkness walked	20	15	○			◐	
The star of heaven foretells	138			○		○	
The Truth from above –							
see Christ is the Truth sent from above							
The virgin Mary had a baby boy	121		○	○	○		
There's a Saviour to see	108			○		○	
This endris nyght I saw a sight –							
see Behold, the great Creator makes							
and From east to west, from shore to shore							
This is the Truth sent from above –							
see Christ is the Truth sent from above							
Thou must leave thy lowly dwelling –							
see Jesus, child of gentle Mary							
Thou whom shepherds worshipped hearing –							
see Shepherds came, their praises bringing							
Three kings from Persian lands afar	136			○		○	
Thy kingdom come! On bended knee –							
see Your kingdom come							
To Bethlehem the strangers came	32			○		○	

Title	CFT	Supp	Cong	Anth	Unis	SATB	Instr
To us in Bethlem city –							
see The Lord of life and glory							
Travellers all to Bethlehem	69			○		○	
Uns ist geborn ein Kindelein –							
see Jesus Christ the Lord is born							
Unto us a boy is born –							
see Jesus Christ the Lord is born							
Up, good Christen folk and listen –							
see Wake then, Christian, come and listen							
Veni, Redemptor genitum –							
see O come, our world's Redeemer, come							
Veni, veni Emmanuel –							
see O come, O come, Emmanuel							
Vom Himmel hoch –							
see From highest heaven where praises ring							
Vox clara ecce intonat –							
see Hark! a trumpet call is sounding							
W zlobie lezy –							
see Infant holy, infant lowly							
Wachet auf, ruft uns die Stimme –							
see Wake, O wake, and sleep no longer							
Wake, O wake, and sleep no longer	10		○	○		○	
Wake then, Christian, come and listen	76			○		○	
We hail the approaching God	16	83	○			○	●
We three kings of Orient are	139		○	○		○	
What child is this	133	58	○	●	●	○	
When came in flesh the incarnate Word							
(Bellman's Carol)	81		○	○		○	
When came in flesh the incarnate Word (St Stephen)	82		○			○	
When God from heaven to earth came down	100	90	○	○		○	●
When the angel came to Mary	26	71		◐		○	
Where is this stupendous stranger (Kit Smart)	132			○	○		
Where is this stupendous stranger (Lismore)	131			○		○	
While shepherds watched their flocks	77	87	○			○	●
Wie schön leuchtet der Morgenstern –							
see How brightly gleams the morning star							
Willie, take your little drum –							
see Bethlehem, we come to bring							
Within this humble manger lies	53			○		○	
Word of the Father everlasting	163		○	○		○	
You servants of the Lord	9	81	○			○	●
You were a child of mine	183			○	○		
Your kingdom come	4	79	○			○	●
Zither Carol –							
see Girls and boys, leave your toys							
Zu Bethlehem geboren –							
see The Lord of life and glory							